I HEARD THE VOICE

I HEARD
THE VOICE

A Compendium of Sussex Hymnody

P. A. J. HODGKINSON

First Edition 2018

Sussex adapted and arranged by Ralph Vaughan Williams (1872-
1958) from *The English Hymnal*. Reproduced by permission of
Oxford University Press. All rights reserved.

Monks Gate English traditional melody collected, adapted and
arranged by Ralph Vaughan Williams (1872-1958) from *The English
Hymnal*. Reproduced by permission of Oxford University Press. All
rights reserved.

Rodmell and *Rustington* are reproduced by permission of The
Canterbury Press, Norwich. *Wadhurst* is reproduced by kind
permission of the Trustees of the Tippett Estate. Images of the
Journal of the Folk-Song Society are reproduced with authorization.

I am extremely grateful to the Bishop of Chichester for his
Foreword. Thanks also to James Bartlett, Serenhedd James, The
Salvation Army, the Michael Tippett Musical Foundation, the
English Folk Dance and Song Society (formerly the Folk-Song
Society), and Martin from Wadhurst.

The cover photograph is of St Peter's Church, Rodmell.

To the hearty hymn-singers of Sussex

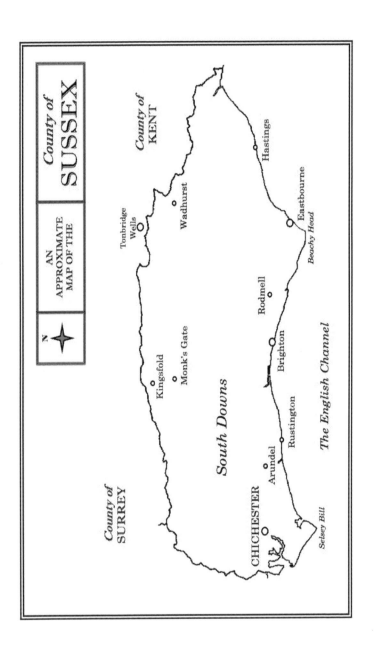

County of
SUSSEX

AN
APPROXIMATE
MAP OF THE

N

County of
KENT

County of
SURREY

Tonbridge
Wells

Wadhurst

Hastings

Eastbourne

Beachy Head

Rodmell

Monk's Gate

Kingsfold

Brighton

South Downs

Rustington

The English Channel

Arundel

CHICHESTER

Selsey Bill

Contents

Foreword 3

Sussex by the sea 5

Vaughan Williams 11

SUSSEX 17

MONKS GATE 21

THE SUSSEX CAROL 25

KINGSFOLD 31

RODMELL 41

RUSTINGTON 45

WADHURST 51

Index of Hymns 56

References 57

Foreword

The Rt Revd Dr Martin Warner
Lord Bishop of Chichester

The rattle of trains and the roar of motor traffic now envelop the ancient county of Sussex with a clamour that generally makes its older, indigenous sounds more difficult to hear. These are the unchanging sounds of the landscape and its coastal border, and they can still haunt and stimulate the imagination.

One expression of an imaginative response to the land and sea is the early medieval decorative detail that we see in the carvings and wall paintings of some astonishingly well-preserved churches. *I Heard the Voice* invites us also to rediscover the music inspired in a bygone age by this rustic county. This compendium connects past and present as it documents the origin of familiar hymn tunes in a much older tradition.

This is an enchanting, compelling collection, and a well-informed guide to the hidden life of Sussex. It is an account that might also prompt connection with another reality: the music of heaven, made familiar to us by distant echoes in our hymnody on earth.

✠ MARTIN CICESTR:

Sussex by the sea

God gives all men all earth to love,
But since man's heart is small,
Ordains for each one spot shall prove
Beloved over all.
Each to his choice, and I rejoice
The lot has fallen to me
In a fair ground – in a fair ground –
Yea, Sussex by the sea!

Sussex, Rudyard Kipling (1902)

The county of Sussex – now divided into the ceremonial counties of East Sussex and West Sussex – has been continuously alive with music for three millennia. A Bronze Age horn, thought to date from around 900BC, was spotted at the bottom of a well in Battle, East Sussex, in the late 1700s. The 14th-century Robertsbridge Codex, from the village near the Sussex-Kent border, includes one of the earliest known pieces written specifically for keyboard; and it is highly likely that the 16th-century Caius and Lambeth Choirbooks

– containing of some of the most important surviving Tudor church music in England – originated in Arundel, the charming West Sussex market town.

Just down the road in Chichester, composer Thomas Weelkes (1576-1623) was Organist and *Informator Choristarum* of the county's Anglican cathedral. Despite his reputation as a foul-mouthed, weak-bladdered* drunkard, Weelkes composed madrigals and liturgical pieces of the highest quality, many of which are still firmly in the canon.

Over three centuries after Weelkes, Revd Walter Hussey, Dean of Chichester, commissioned for the cathedral several of the most important choral works of the 20th

---

* Best not to ask.

century, including Bernstein's *Chichester Psalms.** Debussy famously completed his popular orchestral work *La Mer* (1905) at the Grand Hotel on the seafront at Eastbourne; Elgar composed the celebrated *Cello Concerto, op. 85* in his woodland studio at Fittleworth, West Sussex, in 1919; and, in 1934, John Christie established an opera festival at Glyndebourne.

---

* In his previous post as Vicar of St Matthew's, Northampton, Hussey commissioned several more of the greatest pieces of the repertory, including Finzi's *Lo, the full final sacrifice* and Britten's *Rejoice in the Lamb*. He also commissioned artwork by Henry Moore, Graham Sutherland, John Piper and Marc Chagall. The man was remarkable. There is an amusing anecdote regarding payment for the Bernstein commission. LB travelled to Chichester for the English première; after lunch in the Deanery, Hussey wrang his hands nervously and said something along the lines of 'Lenny, I'm all too aware we haven't discussed the matter of payment', to which Bernstein replied 'oh, don't worry about that', presumably meaning that lunch wasn't the time to talk about money. Hussey took this to mean that Bernstein would waive a fee entirely: 'oh thank you, Leonard, most kind!' he exclaimed. And so the *Chichester Psalms* was completely free!

In centuries past, the breeze across the Downs carried the unbroken hum of countless folk songs. Distinguished Horsham resident Henry Burstow (1826-1916) – cobbler, bell ringer, local historical author, and folk-song enthusiast – had an astonishing 420 songs in his repertoire.[i] A great number of 'Sussex' folk songs, many of which have origins or variants in other counties, have been formally collected, perhaps first by the Revd John Broadwood, who published *Old English songs – as now sung by the Peasantry of the Weald of Surrey and Sussex* in 1843.

The gentle towns and villages that envelop the Downs and gaze out across the Channel offer the melodies and memories of yesteryear, affording inspiration for the creativity of succeeding generations. From Sussex came many of Ralph Vaughan Williams' best-loved melodies, along with original hymns by other notable 20th-century denizens, Hubert Parry (of JERUSALEM) and Michael Tippett.

This short volume may be of some interest to musicians, or poets, or church-goers (committed and lapsed), or local historians, or residents of Sussex, or indeed anyone with an interest in the origins of some of the greatest hymn tunes ever written. I have tried to be varied in my portraits so as to appeal to as broad a readership as possible, and to prevent any risk through boredom of snoozing or premature death. Thus, readers will find some musical analysis, some contextual history, some architectural description, and much fanciful embellishment. I hope this combination will not be found too disagreeable.

Vaughan Williams

Ah! hills beloved! –
    where once, a happy child,
Your beechen shades,
    your turf, your flowers among,
I wove your bluebells
    into garlands wild,
And woke your echoes
    with my artless song.

Sonnet V: To the South Downs
Charlotte Turner Smith (1795)

The preeminent English composer Ralph Vaughan Williams (1872-1958) is perhaps most established in the public consciousness thanks to his 1914 work for violin, *The Lark Ascending*, as well as his notable contribution to music for the church, its hymnody in particular. He was keenly aware of the shadow cast by the bygone giants of English music. His style was informed by that of his canonical predecessors, especially Thomas Tallis (c.1505-1585), and many of his compositions are rooted in the traditional folk music of the British Isles.

In the early 20th-century, for around a month per year for a decade, the composer traversed the country, sipping warm beer in deep-thatched hostelries, listening to weather-worn locals humming tunes passed down from their forebears.* He collected a vast number of folk songs from 21 English counties, most of them from Essex, Norfolk, Herefordshire, and Sussex.

At the turn of the century, the Victorian zeal for collecting and cataloguing anything and everything – from Elgin's marble masterpieces to Darwin's flora and fauna – endured. In 1899, a group of musicians, including Cecil Sharp, Percy Grainger, George Butterworth, and Vaughan Williams himself, founded the Folk-Song Society, both out of a love for the genre and a concern that the tradition was becoming increasingly lost with succeeding generations. Hubert Parry gave the address at the inaugural conference.

---

* *The South Country* by Sussex poet Hilaire Belloc is rather appropriate, particularly the last ten lines. Worth looking up.

This band of young enthusiasts recorded hundreds upon hundreds of folk songs from local sources, using manuscript and, sometimes, a phonograph – a primitive recording device.

In an article from the 1908 edition of the *Journal of the Folk-Song Society*, Grainger reports the reaction of one of his subjects to the Standard Edison Bell Phonograph:

> An old singer, on hearing a long song of his repeated by the phonograph, said: 'He's learnt that quicker nor I'.[ii]

The use of folk song in his own music satisfied Vaughan Williams' desire for a tangible connection with the musical past, and his lifelong vocation to make music accessible to as wide an audience as possible. He noted that in generations gone it was quite common for composers to 'recycle' well-known tunes – from plainsong to popular melodies – as a basis for or feature of their original compositions.

In 1904, Vaughan Williams was asked to contribute to and be musical editor of a major new hymn book, *The English Hymnal* (1906; rev. 1933). Whilst he was certainly a fixture of the musical establishment, it was perhaps an unusual (and enlightened) decision of the Revd Percy Dearmer to enlist an unabashed atheist* to edit a hymn book – but an excellent choice it proved to be.

The little green book, much in part thanks to RVW's inspired editorial contribution, was musically revolutionary. He kept only the best of the (some might say overly-sentimental) Victoriana that formed the diet of congregational singing at the turn of the century, and added the finest music, both new and old, to form a truly catholic oeuvre. The anthology included plainsong, reformation psalms, and well-known tunes from across the British Isles, the continent, and America.

---

* Later in life, Vaughan Williams described himself as a 'cheerful agnostic'.

To *The English Hymnal,* Vaughan Williams contributed seven original tunes, most notably SINE NOMINE (*For all the Saints who from their labours rest*) and DOWN AMPNEY (*Come down, O Love divine*). In a marriage of sacred and secular, he also adapted over forty traditional folk songs, many of which can be counted amongst the most dearly loved hymns of this country and beyond. Perhaps the most familiar example is FOREST GREEN, the tune for *O little town of Bethlehem,* which began as the melody of a folk song from Surrey, *The Ploughboy's Dream.* Two others that may be considered in the same breath are MONKS GATE (*He who would valiant be*) and KINGSFOLD (*I heard the voice of Jesus say*), both collected in Sussex.

> '...a feeling of recognition, as of meeting an old friend, which comes to us all in the face of great artistic experiences. I had the same experience when I first heard an English folksong, when I first saw Michelangelo's Day and Night, when I suddenly came upon Stonehenge or had my first sight of New York City - the intuition that I had been there already.'
>
> Ralph Vaughan Williams

SUSSEX

Father, hear the prayer we offer

In 1904, the same year he was commissioned as an editor of *The English Hymnal*, Vaughan Williams paid a visit to Peter and Harriet Verrall, just outside Horsham. The Verralls were keen singers who would sit around the fire of an evening enjoying songs from Harriet's vast library of folk tunes.

Amongst this collection was *The Royal George*, a folk song about a tragic shipwreck. Vaughan Williams was to hear this song again in Southwold, Suffolk a few years later, there known as *The loss of the Royal George*.

HMS Royal George was a 100-gun Royal Navy ship which, at the time of her launch in 1756, was the largest warship in the world. The ship sank in Portsmouth in 1782 as a result of a miscalculation by a maintenance man, with the loss of many lives. Subsequently, several of the cannons were salvaged and melted down and used for the reliefs around the base of Nelson's Column in Trafalgar Square.

> As we set sail from the rock of Gibraltar,
> As we set sail for sweet Dublin Bay,
> Little did we think of our sad misfortune,
> A-sleeping in the briny sea.
>
> *The Royal George,* Trad.

The tune of this unhappy tale was harmonised and set to a religious text of Maria Willis (1824-1908), a fine example of Vaughan Williams' skill in the convincing cross-pollination of secular and sacred. Both melody and harmony match Willis' text extremely comfortably.

The first half of each verse (apart from the last) of the text tends towards clarifying what the petitioner *isn't* asking for. This is matched in the music by a brief foray into E minor at the end of the first of the two distinct two-bar phrases, and an imperfect cadence at the end of bar 4. This cadence is a kind of musical question mark; it leaves the first half of the hymn obviously unfinished, requiring an answer or clarification in the second part.

By contrast, the second half of each verse – all except the last beginning with the word 'But' – offers more positive action, complete with some potent imagery: 'But the steep and rugged pathway / May we tread rejoicingly' (v2), and 'But would smite the living fountains / From the rocks along our way' (v3). The music here is more poised and triumphant than in the first half. Each bar (apart from the final cadence) begins with a bright and emphatic G major chord, and the contrary motion of the soprano and bass parts at the end of bar 6 lends the latter four bars a sense of being a convincing whole, more so than the first half of the hymn.

MONKS GATE

He who would valiant be

He who would vali - ant be 'Gainst all dis - as - ter,

He who would valiant be
'Gainst all disaster,
Let him in constancy
Follow the Master.
There's no discouragement
Shall make him once relent
His first avowed intent
To be a pilgrim.

The Pilgrim's Progress, John Bunyan (extract)
(ed. Dearmer, 1906)

A short distance from Horsham lies the hamlet of Monks Gate, sometime home of Peter and Harriet Verrall. The two so-called 'Thrift Cottages' are housed in an attractive brick building, its façade rendered white, with a small front garden surrounded by a low, rickety wooden fence.

It was here that Vaughan Williams met the Verralls in 1904, and where they sang to him a great many folk songs, including a tune to texts entitled *Welcome sailor*, or *A blacksmith courted me*, or, as Mrs V. is supposed to have preferred, *Our Captain calls* [or *cries*] *all hands*. Vaughan Williams collected this tune again five years later from a Mrs Powell of Weobley in Herefordshire (he clearly had a way with folk-singing ladies of a certain age). He tied the melody to words of John Bunyan, resulting in the hymn *He who would valiant be* to the tune MONKS GATE.

The text was adapted from Part II of Bunyan's magnum opus, *The Pilgrim's Progress from This World, to That Which Is to Come* (1678). This allegorical work is certainly one of the most significant religious texts of English literature. The hymn recalls the words from the Letter to the Hebrews: '…and confessed that they were strangers and pilgrims on earth'.[iii]

Vaughn Williams was so inspired by this text that he determined to compose an opera based on Bunyan's pilgrim. This proved to be a protracted project, one that he revisited sporadically throughout his life. He used much of the music written for the opera in his Symphony No. 5 (1938), but did eventually complete the work. *The Pilgrim's Progress* was premiered in 1951, and has been revived several times since.

Even to Dearmer's progressive ears, Bunyan's original poetry was deemed too indelicate, so he set about mollifying the language in order to avoid unwarranted stirring in the pews. Perhaps it was the supernatural reference in the third verse to which Percy so objected:

> Hobgoblin nor foul fiend
> Can daunt his spirit,
> He knows he at the end
> Shall life inherit.
> Then fancies fly away,
> He'll fear not what men say,
> He'll labour night and day
> To be a pilgrim.
>
> Bunyan
> (original text, 1678)

THE SUSSEX CAROL
On Christmas night all Christians sing

Tune noted by R. Vaughan Williams, Mus. Doc.

SUNG BY MRS. VERRALL, MONKS GATE, NEAR HORSHAM, SUSSEX, MAY 24TH, 1904.

See "On Christmas night the Joy-bells ring" (No. 28.) Mrs. Verrall sang almost exactly the same words as Mr. Grantham, though fewer verses. Compare the tunes with "Hark, hark the news" in W. Sandys *Christmas Carols*, 1833. The words of both these were still being annually printed up to 1823 on ballad-sheets. (*See* Hone's *Ancient Mysteries*, 1823).—L. E. B.

Journal of the Folk-Song Society, No. 7, Vol. 2 (1905)

On Christmas night all Christians sing
To hear the news the angels bring.
News of great joy, news of great mirth,
News of our merciful King's birth.

Published by Bishop Wadding (1684)

C arry on a mile down the road from Monks Gate and you will find, just past the timber-framed Black Horse Inn, the delightful church of St Andrew in the village of Nuthurst.

Enter through the elaborate lych-gate into the vast churchyard and you will see ahead this attractive church, crowned with a simple wood-clad spire. On the outside of the church, there is evidence of a Norman window on the north chancel wall, as well as two lancets from the 13th century.

The church was rebuilt and altered in 1887 and again in 1907, and now looks, to all intents and purposes, like a Victorian building. Of particular note inside the church is the unusual Elizabethan 'Dole Cupboard', once used for storing bread. A local benefactor, Richard Lewkas, instituted in 1558 that his descendants should 'deliver a cowe to the churchwardens of Nuthurst...once a year...with bred and beer for the poor people'.[iv] I am informed that, regrettably, the churchwardens no longer dole out these tasty treats.

The simplicity of the nave is in contrast to the impressive carving and painting in the chancel and sanctuary, which include a decorative rood screen and a pair of painted organ cases.

Below these cases lie the humble choir stalls. The church almanac of 1895 notes that there was a choir of twenty; so it may be that Mr and Mrs Verrall of Monks Gate, keen singers as they were, made up ten per cent of their local church choir.* Nor is it beyond the realm of possibility that this choir counted the now-celebrated SUSSEX CAROL amongst its festive repertory. This was another tune sung to Vaughan Williams by Harriet Verrall, in May 1904.

Although rarely sung congregationally, the carol remains popular with choirs. The earliest published record (of a slightly altered version) of the text can be found in *Small Garland of Pious and Godly Songs,* printed in 1684. Lucy Broadwood (1858-1929) collected a version of the text to a different tune in Holmwood, Surrey, in 1892, and James Cooksey Culwick (1845-1907) noted yet another tune in South Staffordshire.[v]

---

* This is pure conjecture. They might well have been Methodists for all I know.

But it is Vaughan Williams' account from Sussex that is preponderate, largely owing to its inclusion in his ever-popular *Fantasia on Christmas Carols*, written for the Three Choirs Festival in 1912. Subsequent arrangements by David Willcocks and Philip Ledger have become widespread since their first broadcasts from King's College, Cambridge.

KINGSFOLD

I heard the voice of Jesus say

I heard the voice of Jesus say,
'Come unto me and rest;
Lay down, thou weary one, lay down
Thy head upon my breast':
I came to Jesus as I was,
Weary, and worn, and sad;
I found in him a resting-place,
And he has made me glad.

Horatius Bonar (1846)

On the old Dorking Road, not far from Leith Hill – after which the festival founded by Margaret Vaughan Williams, the composer's sister, is named – sits a public house called The Owl at Kingsfold, known in Vaughan Williams' time as The Wheatsheaf. It was here in December 1904, perhaps as he stopped off for a refreshing ale by the fire after a visit to Monks Gate, that he heard a version of the folk song that would become one of his greatest hymn tunes.

Overleaf: from *English County Songs*,
ed. Broadwood and Fuller Maitland (1893)

Lazarus.

[MIDDLESEX.

J. A. F. M.

1. As
it fell out up - on one day, Rich Di - ver - us he made a
feast; And he in - vit - ed all his friends, And gen - try of the
best. And it fell out up - on one day, Poor La - za - rus he was so
poor, He came and laid him down and down, Ev'n down at Di - ver - us'

Andantino.

(102)

32

LAZARUS.

door, And it fell out up-on one day, Poor La-za-rus he was so

poor, He came and laid him down and down, Ev'n down at Di-ver-us' door.

dim. *pp* *rall.*

1 As it fell out upon one day.
  Rich Diverus he made a feast;
And he invited all his friends,
  And gentry of the best.
And it fell out upon one day,
  Poor Lazarus he was so poor,
He came and laid him down and down,
  Ev'n down at Diverus' door.

2 So Lazarus laid him down and down,
  Ev'n down at Diverus' door;
" Some meat, some drink, brother Diverus,
  Do bestow upon the poor."
" Thou art none of mine, brother Lazarus,
  Lying begging at my door,
No meat, no drink will I give thee,
  Nor bestow upon the poor."

3 Then Lazarus laid him down and down,
  Ev'n down at Diverus' wall;
" Some meat, some drink, brother Diverus,
  Or surely starve I shall."
" Thou art none of mine, brother Lazarus,
  Lying begging at my wall;
No meat, no drink will I give thee,
  And therefore starve thou shall."

4 Then Lazarus laid him down and down,
  Ev'n down at Diverus' gate;
" Some meat, some drink, brother Diverus,
  For Jesus Christ his sake."

" Thou art none of mine, brother Lazarus,
  Lying begging at my gate,
No meat, no drink will I give thee,
  For Jesus Christ his sake."

5 Then Diverus sent his merry men all,
  To whip poor Lazarus away;
They had not power to whip one whip,
  But threw their whips away.
Then Diverus sent out his hungry dogs,
  To bite poor Lazarus away;
They had not power to bite one bite,
  But licked his sores away.

6 And it fell out upon one day,
  Poor Lazarus he sickened and died;
There came two angels out of heaven,
  His soul thereto to guide.
" Rise up, rise up, brother Lazarus,
  And come along with me,
There is a place prepared in heaven,
  For to sit upon an angel's knee."

7 And it fell out upon one day,
  Rich Diverus sickened and died;
There came two serpents out of hell
  His soul thereto to guide.
" Rise up, rise up, brother Diverus,
  And come along with me ;
There is a place prepared in hell,
  For to sit upon a serpent's knee."

(The tune noted by A. J. Hipkins, Esq., F.S.A., in Westminster; the words from *Notes and Queries*, Ser. 4, vol. iii., 76.)

It is not claimed that these words belong to the beautiful tune here given, but they suit it so well that there is a great probability of their having at one time been associated together. Mr. Hipkins knew no words for the tune, but has known it for many years under the name " Lazarus:" it was also recognized as the tune belonging to a song referring to the same subject, by an old woman in Westminster, in December, 1892. The last verse is quoted by Hone (*Every Day Book*, vol. i., p. 1598) as being still sung in 1826 in Warwickshire. The writer in *Notes and Queries* who gives it in extenso, as above, calls it a Worcestershire Carol. See also Husk's *Songs of the Nativity*, " Dives and Lazarus," where three more stanzas are given. In the above version the form Diverus is always sung ; and the same form is alluded to in Fletcher's *Monsieur Thomas* [1639]. In Beaumont and Fletcher's *Nice Valour*, act iv., sc. 1, " Dives " is spoken of as one of the ballads hanging at church corners. The tune should be compared with "The Thresher" (p. 68), and with "Cold blows the wind" (p. 34), as well as with "We are frozen-out gardeners," in Chappell's *Popular Music*. The tune strongly resembles " Gilderoy," see notes to "Cold blows the wind" (p. 34).

(103)

It is uncertain whether this was the first time Vaughan Williams had heard the tune, or if the rendition in The Wheatsheaf served purely as a reminder. Some sources suggest he knew of it, or a similar version (for there are many) as a youngster. A feature in the *Journal of the Folk-Song Society* (1905) states that the tune can be found attached to a ballad known as *Gilderoy*, published in 1719 in the (gloriously named) collection *D'Urfey's Pills to Purge Melancholy*.[vi]

The tune we recognise now was first published in a volume entitled *English County Songs*, compiled in 1893 by Lucy Broadwood (of the piano manufacturing family) and John Fuller Maitland. A Broadwood's employee, Alfred Hipkins, who knew the tune as *Lazarus*, passed it onto Lucy. Hipkins did not know the text, so for her publication Broadwood married this melody with the biblical story of Dives and Lazarus, in the form of a ballad. This is the title Vaughan Williams adopted for his 1939 work for harp and string orchestra which takes the melody as its theme, *Five Variants of Dives and Lazarus*.

The version that Vaughan Williams heard in The Wheatsheaf, sung by a Mr Booker, tells a typically hopeless tale; this time of a gruesome murder in Suffolk in 1827, *The Ballad of Maria Marten* [or *Martin*]. Maria's lover, William Corder, persuaded her to elope with him to Ipswich (who could refuse?). They met under the cover of darkness at the Red Barn in Polstead, not far from her family farm, whence they were to flee together.*

Over the next few weeks, Corder sent letters to Maria's father telling him they were safe and well on the Isle of Wight. At that same time, Maria's stepmother suffered several nightmares, and persuaded her husband to search the barn.

---

* I recently drove past a sign to Polstead unexpectedly, and couldn't resist turning off. In the centre of the village lies 'Corder's House'; venture down Marten's Lane and you will find a farmhouse called 'Maria Marten's'. The Red Barn is no longer there as it was destroyed by fire. On a hilltop high above the village sits the parish church of St Mary (unusually Norman for Suffolk). Maria was buried in the churchyard in 1827 but, sadly, her headstone has long-since been destroyed by what the church guidebook describes as 'rapacious souvenir hunters'.

He found his daughter's body in a shallow grave; she had been shot. Corder swung for the murder, and the story captured the public imagination with such fervour that it inspired numerous articles, plays, and songs, such as this ballad.[*]

'If you will meet me at the Red Barn
  as sure as I have life,
I will take you to Ipswich town
  and there make you my wife.'

He straight went home and fetched his gun,
  his pickaxe and his spade,
He went into the Red Barn,
  and there he dug her grave.

The Ballad of Maria Marten, Trad. (extract)

---

[*] In his iconic tome *England's Thousand Best Churches,* Simon Jenkins reveals that there were over 10,000 spectators at the hanging, and, rather gruesomely, the authorities bound the trial records in the guilty man's skin.

IV.—Maria Martin."

SUNG BY MR. BOOKER,
ÆOLIAN.   AT THE "WHEATSHEAF," KINGSFOLD, SUSSEX, DEC. 23RD, 1904.

The Mixolydian and Æolian or Dorian tunes to these words are really variants of the same tune, being almost identical in outline, except for the major third in the Mixolydian tune, and the minor in the Dorian and Æolian.

There seems to be some subtle connection between the words of " Maria Martin " and " Come all you worthy Christians," as they are so often sung to variants of the same tune.—R. V. W.

Journal of the Folk-Song Society, No.7, Vol. 2 (1905)

In a 1905 volume of the *Journal of the Folk-Song Society* , Vaughan Williams noted four tunes that he had heard associated with *The Ballad of Maria Marten*. Three are recognisable as variations of the melody we know as KINGSFOLD (two from Tilney All Saints, Norfolk, and the other from Kingsfold itself), and another quite different tune that he collected from the Verralls.[vii]

An Irish text associated with yet another version of the tune, *Star of the County Down*, is rather more optimistic than the Suffolk tale:

Near Banbridge town, in the County Down,
    One morning last July,
Down a bóthrín green came a sweet cailín,
    And she smiled as she passed me by.*

The hymn tune (as published in *The English Hymnal*) and Vaughan Williams' harmony are, for me at least, somewhat musically inconclusive. The melody has a melancholic disposition, partly cultivated by the modality, and partly by the wilt at the end of every phrase, each one finishing – both melodically and harmonically – lower than it begins. The harmony reads as a tussle between the bright G major and the mournful Aeolian mode on E, neither tonal form ever gaining outright authority.

The performer or listener might be left with an impression that there *is* a cordial conclusion, but that it lies somewhere just out of reach.

---

* A 'bóthrín' is a rural lane; a 'cailín' is a young woman.

The text of the hymn was written by Scottish pastor Horatius Bonar (1808-1889), soon after the Church of Scotland schism in 1843. This must have been an intensely painful and testing time for the good-hearted cleric.

> I heard the voice of Jesus say,
> 'I am this dark world's Light:
> Look unto me, thy morn shall rise,
> And all thy day be bright'.

For the feast of the Holy Innocents
December 28ᵗʰ

When Christ was born in Bethlehem,
    Fair peace on earth to bring,
In lowly state of love he came
    To be the children's King.

A mother's heart was there his thrown,
    His orb a maiden's breast,
Whereby he made through love alone
    His kingdom manifest.

And round him, then, a holy band
    Of children blest was born,
Fair guardians of his throne to stand
    Attendant night and morn.

&c.

Laurence Housman (1865-1959)

RODMELL
When Christ was born in Bethlehem

Vaughan Williams was fervent in his mission to make music as accessible to as many people as possible. He chose not to sit secluded in an ivory tower, scribbling away on manuscript, but instead used his talents as publicly as he could, as a composer, teacher, conductor, adjudicator, and editor of a national hymnal. He believed very strongly in a cultural democracy, and that music in particular should transcend boundaries of social class and artistic acumen.*

Having been a church organist for a time, Vaughan Williams understood the strengths and limitations of both amateur choirs and congregations. Much of his small corpus of liturgical choral music was written with the limited resources of the parish choir in mind,

---

* Hubert Parry, RVW's composition teacher at the Royal College of Music, instructed him to go and write choral music like an Englishman and a democrat. These words were clearly not lost!

and many of his choral hymn arrangements, for example *O God our help in ages past* and *All people that on earth do dwell* give equal credence to choir and congregation. His music often gives the congregation a voice with which they can contribute to the musical elements of a service on an equal footing with the choir.

The use of popular folk tunes in and of itself is an indication of Vaughan Williams' regard for congregational participation, as is the emphasis and care he placed on pitch, range, and melody – many tunes were simplified, and he often instructed them to be sung in unison. RODMELL, originally the melody of a folk song entitled *The Bailiff's Daughter*, is a fine example. In common with his other translations of folk songs for use in church, Vaughan Williams cleansed the tune of any extraneous decoration and ensured a strict strophic format, without the melodic deviation that often occurred in latter verses of the folk versions. Typically, his harmony is entirely diatonic and moves sturdily in even crotchets, providing gentle and reliable support to the all-important melody.

The devastatingly beautiful village of Rodmell lies at the foot of the Downs, on the flood plain of the River Ouse. St Peter's Church is hidden away down a small thoroughfare off the main street, next to a village school so petite it could moonlight on a model railway set at weekends. Six mature yews keep sentry around church, between which one can glimpse the 12th-century tower, crowned with a spire that gleams in the afternoon sunlight. The organ within is a pleasant instrument of seven stops, including a velvety Open Diapason, built in 1908. Vaughan Williams may well have been acquainted with its chorus.

Praise the Rock of our salvation

Tune: Rustington

C. Hubert H. Parry

RUSTINGTON
Praise the Rock of our salvation

Praise the Rock of our salvation,
Laud His name from zone to zone;
On that rock the Church is builded,
Christ himself the corner-stone;
Vain against our rock-built Zion
Winds and waters, fire and hail;
Christ is in her midst; against her
Sin and hell shall not prevail.

Benjamin Webb (1872)

Charles Hubert Hastings Parry was a composer who, unlike Vaughan Williams, was in deep sympathy with the Germanic symphonic tradition. Such was his repute in his lifetime that a portrait made it onto a Wills' Cigarettes card. Today Parry's superlative orchestral output is less well known than the (equally good) choral music; performances of *Blest pair of Sirens* (1887), the *Songs of Farewell* (1915), and *I was glad*, written for the coronation of Edward VII in 1902, are frequent.

Yet it is through his hymn tunes that his work has found a national recognition and admiration. REPTON (*Dear Lord and Father of mankind*) has been a firm favourite since George Gilbert Stocks of Repton School, Derbyshire, extracted Parry's tune from the oratorio *Judith* (1887/8) and wed it to some (superb) verses from a rather long and bizarre text of the American temperance movement, John Greenleaf Whittier's *The Brewing of Soma*. Its place in the national psyche has been strengthened thanks to its inclusion in the 2007 film adaptation of Ian McEwan's novel *Atonement*. JERUSALEM, to Blake's text, remains a favourite of blushing brides, school chapels, rugby terraces, and Proms audiences alike.*

After a bout of ill-health in 1880, Parry moved to the coastal village of Rustington, where he built a large residence known as Knightscroft.

---

* Parry may have composed some or all of JERUSALEM at Rustington, but it is more likely to have been written in London. However, we can be sure that William Blake (1757-1827) wrote the famous text to that hymn in Felpham, West Sussex, in 1804.

For the remainder of his life he divided his time between London (he was Director of the Royal College of Music from 1895 until his death in 1918), Oxford (where he held a professorship, 1900-08), and Rustington.

Rustington has other notable connections: J. M. Barrie, author of *Peter Pan*, was a regular visitor to the Llewellyn Davies family, Rustington residents on whom the Darlings were supposedly modelled; several prominent members of the Suffragist movement, whose efforts Parry wholeheartedly supported, lived in the village; and there is a passing reference to 'Rustington-on-Sea' in *The Gnu Song* by Flanders and Swann.

Parry named three of his original hymn tunes after West Sussex villages: AMBERLEY, ANGMERING, and RUSTINGTON. The last was published in the *Westminster Abbey Hymn Book* (1897), setting words by Benjamin Webb. It is Parry in typically rousing, patriotic form; the ascending motif in the suspension-ridden third line is particularly stirring.

It is now more often sung to *Ye who know the Lord is gracious* (as printed in *The New English Hymnal*), although I rather like Webb's text, zones and all.

Unto the Hills

Tune: Wadhurst

John Campbell (Psalm 121)　　　　　　　　　　　　　　　Michael Tippett

Un - to the hills a-round do I___ lift up My long-ing eyes; O

whence for me shall my sal - va - tion come, From whence a - rise? From

God, the Lord, does come my cer - tain aid,___ From

God, the Lord who Heaven and earth hath made.

WADHURST
Unto the hills around do I lift up

Unto the hills around do I lift up
   My longing eyes;
O whence for me shall my salvation come,
   From whence arise?
From God, the Lord does come
   My certain aid,
From God, the Lord who Heaven
   And earth hath made.

John Campbell (1877)

I should be extremely surprised if you have ever sung this tune beyond the bounds of the pretty market town after which it is named.* I'd wager that the vast majority of my most accomplished church-musically-inclined chums would be reduced to an embarrassed silence if ever they were asked to whistle WADHURST.**

---

* Unless you were a member of the BBC Singers in 2005, in which case you will have recorded it as part of a Tippett album.
** Martin, a guide I met in Wadhurst Parish Church, pronounces it 'Waddust'.

English composer Michael Tippett (1905-98) – neither prolific nor particularly well-known until later in his life – moved to Tidebrook Manor, just outside Wadhurst, in 1951. Each Christmas, Tippett would welcome the band of the Wadhurst Corps of the Salvation Army to Tidebrook to play carols, in exchange for mince pies and (one assumes) cinnamon tea. During the performances in the large wood-panelled hall, Tippett would keep a safe distance, placing himself at the top of the stairs, claiming he could better hear the instrumental balance from there.[viii]

The band was led by George Mallion, proprietor of the local fish shop. After one performance in 1954, during an animated conversation about their favourite carols, Mallion suggested that Tippett should write a congregational hymn for the Salvation Army. The resulting tune, WADHURST, was published in the July-August 1958 edition of *The Musical Salvationist*, setting John Douglas Sutherland Campbell's version of Psalm 121.

I dearly hope that I am not alone in thinking this tune is an absolute gem. Of course, the counterintuitive rhythms, irregular phrases, disjunct vocal part-writing, and, most alarmingly, pitch (good luck with those top G flats on a Sunday morning!) deem it entirely unsuitable for use as a congregational hymn. But as a standalone miniature it is extremely attractive.

It contains several stylistic features one might expect from this 20th-century composer but is devoid of any aggressive discord. Instead, the undulating contours of both melody and harmony gradually and gently lift one's longing eyes up to the hills; certainly to the ridge-tops of the High Weald, if not the divine hills beyond.

Journal

of the

Folk=Song Society.

No. 7

Being the Second Part of Vol. II.

FOLK-SONG SOCIETY.

Balance Sheet, January 1st, 1905, to May 31st, 1905.

Dr.	£	s.	d.	£	s.	d.	Cr.	£	s.	d.	£	s.	d.
1905, Jan. 1st.							1905, May 31st.						
To Balance brought forward :							*By Printing of Journals ...	57	9	7			
In Treasurer's hands ...	63	1	8				„ Postage, Stationery and						
In Hon. Secretary's hands	18	1	7				Carriage	7	14	6			
				81	3	3					65	4	1
							„ Balance carried forward :						
							In Hon. Treasurer's						
							hands	13	19	9			
1905, May 31st.							In Hon. Secretary's						
To Subscriptions received ...	...	30	19	6			hands	52	3	9			
„ Sales of Journals and Leaflets	..	19	4	10							66	3	6
	£131	7	7					£131	7	7			

FOLK-SONG SOCIETY.

LIST OF OFFICERS.

DECEMBER, 1905.

President:

THE RIGHT HON. LORD TENNYSON, G.C.M.G.

Vice-Presidents:

SIR ALEXANDER C. MACKENZIE, Mus. Doc., F.R.A.M.
Principal of the Royal Academy of Music.

SIR C. HUBERT H. PARRY, Bart., Mus. Doc., D.C.L., C.V.O.
Professor of Music in the University of Oxford : Director of the Royal College of Music.

SIR CHARLES VILLIERS STANFORD, Mus. Doc., D.C.L.
Professor of Music in the University of Cambridge.

Committee:

SIR ERNEST CLARKE, *Chairman.*	FRANK KIDSON, Esq.
WALTER FORD, Esq.	J. A. FULLER MAITLAND, Esq.
Mrs. FRANK W. GIBSON (Miss Eugenie Joachim).	CECIL SHARP, Esq.
	J. TODHUNTER, Esq., M.D.
	GILBERT WEBB, Esq.
A. P. GRAVES, Esq.	RALPH VAUGHAN WILLIAMS, Esq.,
ALFRED KALISCH, Esq.	Mus. Doc.

Hon. Secretary:

MISS LUCY BROADWOOD,
84, Carlisle Mansions, Victoria Street, London, S.W.

Hon. Treasurer:

MRS. LAURENCE GOMME.

Index of Hymns

Listed as found in *The English Hymnal* (1906; rev. 1933), and *The New English Hymnal* (1986).

Tune	EH	NEH
Sussex	385	357
Monks Gate	402	372
The Sussex Carol	-	-
Kingsfold	574	376
Rodmell	611	203
Rustington	-	477
Wadhurst	-	-

References

[i] Henry Burstow, *Reminiscences of Horsham*, (Free Christian Church Book Society, 1911), pp. 114-119.

[ii] Percy Grainger, 'Collecting with the Phonograph', reproduced in the *Journal of the Folk-Song Society*, No. 12, Vol. 3 (1908), pp. 147-162.

[iii] Hebrews 11:13 (King James Version).

[iv] St Andrews Church Nuthurst – A Guide and History (2003).

[v] See *Journal of the Folk-Song Society*, Vol. 2, No. 7 (1905), pp. 126-127.

[vi] Ibid.

[vii] Ibid.

[viii] See article 'Sir Michael and the Army' in *The Salvationist*, No. 616, 7th February 1998 (The Salvation Army, 1998).

38279689R00038

Printed in Poland
by Amazon Fulfillment
Poland Sp. z o.o., Wrocław